To H.T.Y.

PRELUDE on 'ST. COLUMBA'

Irish Melody, 1855

'Where streams of living water flow.'

HENRY G. LEY

OXFORD UNIVERSITY PRESS · MUSIC DEPARTMENT · 44 CONDUIT STREET · LONDON, W. 1

where   the   ver - - dant   pas - - - tures

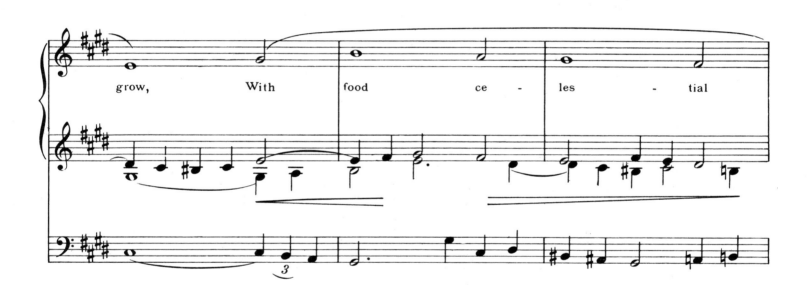

grow,   With   food   ce -   les -   tial

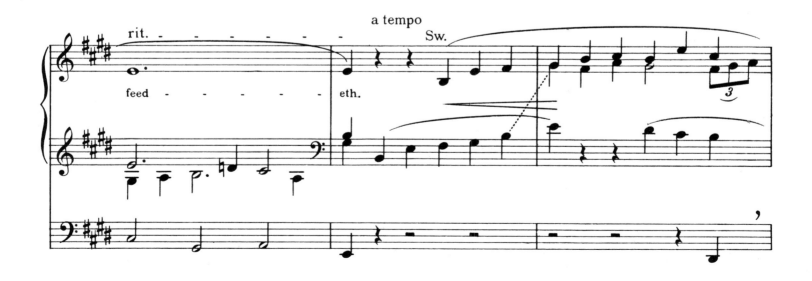

feed - - - - - eth.

4

FANTASIA on 'WAREHAM'

HERBERT MURRILL

6

PRELUDE on 'CHESHIRE'

Prepare:

Sw: Voix Celestes & Salc. 8ft.
Gt: Stopped diap. 8ft. or Soft Flute 8ft.
Ch: Orch. Oboe or Flute 8ft.
Ped: 16ft. & 8ft. coupled to Sw. & Gt.
  (Manuals uncoupled)

GORDON SLATER

10

'PICARDY'

ALEC ROWLEY

13

14

'THIS ENDRYS NIGHT'
A Christmas Pæan

Suggested Registration
  Swell: quiet 8ft. & 4ft.
  Gt. Claribel or soft 8ft.(coupled to Sw.)
  Choir: quiet stops coupled to Sw.
  Pedal: to balance the Manuals

Note: This piece should gradually build up

GEORGE OLDROYD

FINALE on 'HYFRYDOL'

Gt. *mf*
Sw. *mf* coupled to Gt.
Ped. coupled to Sw. and Gt.

HENRY COLEMAN

20

21

Reproduced and printed by
Halstan & Co. Ltd., Amersham, Bucks.

OXFORD UNIVERSITY PRESS